FROM CORPORATE TO CONSULTANT

Pursuing Your Professional Dream

Ellen M. Huxtable, MBA

From Corporate to Consultant

Copyright © 2019 Ellen M. Huxtable

All rights reserved.

ISBN: 9781698608075

To Robert and Nathan Huxtable,
with greatest appreciation
for their ongoing support and
encouragement

From Corporate to Consultant

CONTENTS

1	Welcome!	1
2	Joys and Considerations	3
3	Create Your Concept	7
4	Position to Compete	15
5	Structural Basics	19
6	Human Resources	27
7	Financial Considerations	31
8	Marketing Preparation	37
9	Your Marketing Strategy	43
10	Building Momentum and Beyond	51

1 WELCOME!

If you've ever thought about launching a practice as an independent business consultant, you've landed in the right place. And if you've already decided that independent consulting is for you, this book is a quick and straightforward guide to your new professional world.

The thought of setting out on your own can be both exhilarating and terrifying. On one hand, there are new horizons ahead, with endless vistas of the future you want to create, just waiting for you to seize the opportunities. On the other hand, you might feel like you're getting ready to board a rollercoaster, plummeting into the unknown, surviving and thriving on the experience. Both visions are equally valid.

Take a few moments to reflect on your dreams. Fill in the details of your ideal consultancy practice.

And before boarding the rollercoaster, look ahead. See the tracks from the ground, before you get into the front car and click the harness. Know the twists and turns, the climbs and free falls that are part of making your dreams reality. Consider this book your view from the safety of "what if," rather than the panic of "what now?"

This is an overview and a general guide to the path from corporate to consultant. You and your experiences are unique. Every person has different skills and strengths. Some sections of this book will be basic and repetitive to you; others may require more thought. Specific questions such as the best choice of legal entity depend on a number of factors and are best left to trusted advisors who are familiar with your particular circumstances. Our goal is to alert you to the questions you need to ask, and the issues you need to resolve in taking the next steps.

Take inventory of your strengths, and develop a strong basis for your consulting practice. Set your vision, plan your strategy, and get ready for an amazing ride!

2 JOYS AND CONSIDERATIONS

Entrepreneurship is filled with benefits and considerations, joys and concerns. The joys are the bright shiny promises surrounding self-employment; the concerns are those thoughts that go flickering by just before your fall asleep. Most joys are not transcendent, and most considerations are not deal breakers. But both need to be taken into account as you evaluate independent consulting.

Joys

If you didn't have some idea of the joys of entrepreneurship, you would't be reading this book. Entrepreneurship and independent consulting come with many perks.

- You have control of your schedule. While this can be somewhat limited by the expectations of your clients, you get to make the decisions on when you choose to work. You can opt to spend a weekday with the kids or grandkids, go golfing or shopping or relax on the beach, without worrying about scheduling vacation time in advance.

- You get to make all the decisions; you are in control. You have no boss or board of directors calling the shots or limiting your options. There are no policies with which you disagree. You are free to succeed or fail on your own.

- You can be responsive to client needs. Sometimes the corporate structure presents a challenge to providing service. Decisions might need to be approved by several layers of management, or you might need to get multiple operating units to cooperate in order to fulfill a simple request. As a small business, there is no multi-layer hierarchy, or non-cooperative divisions. You are it, and you can make things happen.

- You can set the goals, purpose, mission, vision and values for your business. Things can be done the way you want, to the standards you set and in conformance to your principles and values. You and the business are one.

- Upward mobility and potential are without limit.

- You can't be fired. You can choose to discontinue the business, but no one can fire you.

Considerations

As you probably suspect, nothing is all sweetness and light. Independent consulting does have its considerations.

- First, are you pursuing a consulting career as a primary source of income, or as a potentially profitable hobby? If as a hobby, some factors are less important. Their impact rises in concert with your financial expectations.

- Be aware, entrepreneurship is a 24/7, 365 days a year proposition. When it's your business, your are always mentally "on the clock."

- There are no paid vacations, holidays, sick time, no group insurance policies or fringe benefits.

- Unlike working in a large corporation, unless you have the expertise, you will need to make provisions, as needed, for IT technical support, legal advice, accounting and related financial tracking, and staffing and staff support.

- Entrepreneurship carries both a time and dollar opportunity cost. You could be spending your time and money on something other than investing in your business.

- Starting a solo practice can be great for concentration and focus, but it can be lonely. There are no co-workers dropping by and no office football pools, birthday parties or baby showers.

- Do recognize the potential impact on family and other relationships. You may be working weekends or late hours, or plans may need to change without notice.

- Cash flow can be boom or bust. Your upward potential is theoretically limitless, but there is no routine payday or safety net. What you kill is what you eat.

- As a rule of thumb, in a fully developed practice, you will be performing billable work one third of the time, marketing your business one third of the time and doing support services, travel and other non-billable activities one third of the time. Twenty hours of billable time will generally equate to a sixty hour workweek.

- Most new businesses take a minimum of two to three years to break even. For a consulting practice, controlling startup costs and marketing strategically can accelerate reaching this milestone.

- There are countless scams and scam artists targeting independent consultants and other small businesses. They exist online and in person. They can present as clients, vendors, advisors and more. Be extremely cautious in establishing your business relationships.

3 CREATE YOUR CONCEPT

While not mandatory, it's generally a good idea to have an idea of where you want to go, and what your business will look like once you get there. What is your vision for your consulting practice? Who do you see as your customer? What exactly will you offer, and how will you deliver your expertise? Who is your competition and how will you effectively compete? When you close your eyes, what is your future vision?

Mission and Vision, Values and Goals

Your business can be anything you want. You set your mission, vision, values and goals. Technically, this is an optional exercise. You can legally establish your business, begin operations and run in perpetuity without ever thinking about these things. By default, your mission will probably be to stay afloat; your vision may be fame and fortune, your values will be whatever your values are, and your goal will likely be to create profit.

Yet giving some consideration to these things can add meaning, direction and purpose to your efforts. Any or all of these factors may change over time, but at any one time, know your aspirations and work toward achieving them.

Your Target Client

Who is your target client? Your first response might be as general as "any business owner," or "any executive," or it may be as specific as "chief financial officers of Fortune 500 companies with last names that begin with the letter Q," or "multinational widget manufacturers in Maine with assets over $500 million."

Carefully consider your target customer. Narrow your focus to those most likely to need your skills, and most willing to pay for your assistance. Research can help you find your personal niche. Poll your contacts in the field. Connect with potential clients and ask what services they need. Practice discernment in assessing feedback. If a contact sees you as a potential competitor or threat, they might be excessively negative toward your concept. On the other hand, friends may be hugely supportive, but ultimately not in a position to engage your services. Learn as much as you can and use this information to structure your business.

- What industry or sector is going to be most receptive to you and your services?

- Is there a timing component to your clients' needs?

- Are there conditions which boost demand for your expertise? For example, would a company have a greater need for you in case of a merger or acquisition, or a union walkout?

- What size of business are you targeting?

- Are there geographic constraints to your service area? What makes sense?

- Are you going to serve clients virtually, in person, or both?

- How many businesses are in your target market? Is the market large enough to be viable?

- Within an organization, who desperately needs what you have to offer? Who will make the hiring decision?

- What pain do you relieve for your client? Is this pain so great that they will be ready to take action?

- And most importantly, will they have the capacity and willingness to pay you, at the rate you are asking, to relieve their pain?

Your Product

You and your expertise are your product. You may have expertise and experience in a broad spectrum of management skills, and can provide service in any of them. What is your strong suit, where you can deliver significant results and meet a critical business need? This should be the focal point of your practice.

Narrow your focus to those clients most likely to engage your services. Strive to be the top of mind, "go to" person for those with a specific, acute pain point. Be the most knowledgeable resource in your field, and the first choice for your targeted clients.

Know what you offer, the pain point you relieve, and your credentials. Be specific. What is your experience? What is your track record? What are your past relevant successes? These are your credentials. Be ready to produce and quantify them. What is the bottom line win? Clients care more about demonstrated achievement than longevity or previous titles. Someone who "increased sales for a current client in this industry by 30% per year for the past three years" is going to gain more traction than than "the senior vice president for sales with 25 years of experience in a company which is no longer active in the marketplace."

Your education and corporate background can also support your position. If you have a relevant degree from a respected university or have served and have references and recommendations from major corporations, these can help prospective clients see you as a valuable resource.

Important note: Do not falsify, exaggerate or make misleading implications about your credentials. The world and the business world are very small, and social media spreads information instantaneously. Your most important product is your integrity. Once this is compromised it is difficult if not impossible to regain.

You are not going to land every potential engagement. Differences in expectations, strategies, personalities or more might steer a prospect to another provider or lead you to decline an opportunity. You will not be the best fit for everyone, but for the right client, strive to be the best and only choice.

What do you have the experience, talent and interest in doing within your business, and what will you outsource? Plan for this both organizationally and in your budget.

Delivery Modes

There are multiple ways in which you can share your expertise.

- Traditional consultative services typically involve a set engagement in which you work with a client to analyze an issue and provide recommendations. These engagements may or may not include implementing the plan.

- Ongoing support typically includes meeting with a client, often on a monthly basis, to provide insight, resources or accountability.

- Group facilitation assists the client by guiding a work group through a decision-making or strategic process.

- Live seminars and workshops can either be self-sponsored or offered through an organization such as a chamber of commerce or trade association.

- Presentations can be virtual or live. These typically run for 30 to 40 minutes or less, to an audience such as a networking group, service organization, or interest group.

- On-line classes can be offered either for free or behind a paywall.

- Blogging can help build visibility and credibility.

- Writing a book or a workbook or ebook (such as this!) can present information to a wider audience.

Depending on your target client and expertise, some modalities are a better fit than others. Different options can compliment each other; for example, a presentation can lead to a traditional engagement, or blogging might lead to the sale of a book.

4 POSITION TO COMPETE

KNOW THE COMPETITION

Who are your competitors? Learn who they are, and as much as you can about their position and strategies. Be focused and proactive, study the field, and gain the edge. Football teams spend hours studying game tapes; your business is at least as important as the weekend's "big game."

- Find your direct competitors. These are individuals or firms offering services similar to yours. Do a google search, mine information from websites and dig into LinkedIn for details.

- Identify indirect competitors. These are the entities which offer alternative solutions to the problems you solve. If you offer team building workshops, your prospects might opt for an escape room experience instead. If you do leadership coaching, targeted clients might forego your services for a membership in an exclusive business roundtable.

- Consider competition from within your prospect's organization. Your targeted client may decide to get help from another department, or an internal mentor, or from polling co-workers during coffee breaks.

- Remember that doing nothing is always an option. It might not be the best option for your prospective client, but it is an option. Procrastination is a fierce competitor.

SET YOUR STRATEGY

Analyze your product, your prospective clients and your competition, and use this information to set your business strategy.

- Evaluate the competition. What do they offer? What are their strong suits, and where are they vulnerable? How are you going to position yourself against them?

- Consider your prospective clients. What do they want? What are their complaints about current offerings? What is on their wish list?

- What do your prospective clients want, that competitors do not offer, that you can provide?

Get creative and set your Unique Selling Proposition.

Your Unique Selling Proposition

Your Unique Selling Proposition (USP) is what sets you above and apart from the competition, and makes you the best choice, if not the only choice, for your targeted client.

Why should a prospect choose to do business with you, and not a competitor? What do you offer that will relieve their pain better, faster, or more completely? How do you differ from everyone else in the field? You need to know this, and share it in your marketing campaigns.

Sometimes what we think makes us unique is really baseline or average. You might say you're unique because "I really care about my clients, and always do what's right for them." Guess what? Every competitor out there can, and probably does, say the same thing. Prospective clients have heard this dozens of times, and you are just one more voice in the crowd. You have to offer more; your USP has to create "wow!"

Your USP might be related to your training, contacts, interests, hobbies, family experiences or a combination of factors. Not everyone knows what you know or has done what you have done. Your USP might hinge on your unique experience, a proprietary process, an innovative delivery system, or deliverable professional connections.

Think through and develop your USP, and use this as the core of your marketing message. Prospective clients will have a range of needs; your USP will attract clients who resonate with your unique competencies.

5 STRUCTURAL BASICS

Your Legal Entity

How are you going to structure your business? Options include a sole proprietorship, partnership, limited liability company, S corporation and C corporation. Each has benefits and restrictions, and your choice depends not only on your current practice, but also on your longer term vision and goals. Your selection of entity can be changed in the future; you are not locked into the decisions you make now.

There are numerous online resources detailing the differences and relative merits of various entities. Websites from government agencies including the Small Business Administration (SBA) and the Small Business Development Centers (SBDCs) can be useful resources in understanding legal entities and other business concerns.

Be aware that as with any online research, some resources provide information from reputable sources while other sources are commercially based and might not deliver services or advice in your best interest.

Locally, a small business lawyer or accountant can give you advice and direction; many of these professionals offer a low cost initial assessment and recommendation. If you do not know one, your local small business banker, chamber of commerce, or Small Business Development Center might be able to suggest professionals.

OTHER LEGALITIES

Depending on your location and business focus, you may need to register your business or meet requirements at the local, county, state or federal level. If you are a sole proprietorship and using a business name, check with your county regarding registering this. Preliminary research can be done online, and a small business lawyer can provide guidance.

The requirement for a tax identification number for your business varies, depending on your entity and designation. As a sole proprietor, you can operate under your social security number. However, this exposes your social security number to wide distribution and potential for misuse. A sole proprietorship can obtain an Employer Identification

Number (EIN) online. For other entities the EIN is done as part of the process of establishing the entity. The Internal Revenue Service website provides detailed information on this.

Your choice of entity has implications for legal exposure. Establishing a corporation can shield you from some, but not necessarily all liability for your business. Under a sole proprietorship, you are liable for your actions and the actions of the company. A partnership arrangement can generate increased exposure, as any partner can obligate the partnership.

Basic Equipment

As with any business, your business will require basic equipment and services. For most consultant services, these can be minimal.

- A reliable computer. This is your lifeline. You need it to access and send emails, do your proposals and reports, do spreadsheets, develop print materials and presentations, engage in social media, update your website, keep your financial records, and much more.

- Software, including word processing, spreadsheets and presentations. Photo editing and graphics software are also highly desirable.

- Email software. Sending mass emails from your personal email account is a violation of the anti-spam laws. If this pattern is identified, your email service can be blocked. Commercial email systems are available which are free or very low cost. These systems have permanent templates to ensure compliance with anti-spam regulations. Individuals you place on your email list must have given their consent; the software gives them the option of opting out and prohibits you from re-adding them.

- Backup for your computer. This can be cloud based, on a separate drive, or both. Backup is critical. In business, you have too much to lose.

- Printer and scanner capability. You will be developing your own proposals and reports.

- A business telephone and number. Keep your business and personal numbers separate. You don't want to give your personal phone number out to vendors and clients.

- A mobile phone. You will need to access information remotely.

- Office supplies.

- A reliable car. As a consultant, you will be on the move. Much if not all of your travel will be local, but the local miles add up. A car in the shop can mean juggling appointments and scrambling to meet obligations.

Facility Options

You can locate your consulting business anywhere from your kitchen table to a downtown office suite.

- A home-based business minimizes commuting time and eliminates office rental expense. It can enable you to blend work and home obligations throughout the day. On the downside, working from home can be distracting and decrease productivity. Home phone calls, doorbells, barking pets and other home based noises may distract from your professionalism during phone or video calls or video presentations. Not all home office configurations can be claimed as a business expense. Check with the IRS website or a small business accountant to assess if this is applicable to you.

- Co-working facilities provide professional shared space and amenities. You may have access to a common work area, or in some cases, the option to rent dedicated space. Private meeting rooms are typically available for client or work group meetings. Co-working facilities may also provide their clients with networking and education opportunities.

- Work space organizations are similar to co-working facilities, and may provide additional services and amenities. These can include receptionist and telephone coverage, private offices and concierge services. Some work space organizations operate a worldwide network of facilities and offer reciprocity between sites.

- Office space sub-rental is the option to lease space within another business. This can be advantageous if you are renting from an organization with synergies to yours. Downsides include the need to accommodate the preferences of your landlord regarding access hours, client traffic or other co-habitation issues. You may incur startup expenses for internet or telephone installation, furnishings or minor decorating.

- Renting or leasing your own space gives you greater control over your environment. You will need to invest in furnishings and possibly decorating, and will need to arrange for services including phone, internet, and, in some cases, utilities. Compared to other options, you may be required to make a longer term commitment for the use of the space.

- Membership in an exclusive club can partner with any location option and give you the capability to meet with and entertain high end clients in an elite setting.

- Coffee shops and cafes are a mainstay of entrepreneurs. They offer a casual, convenient location, with minimal expense. If you use one of these locations for a meeting, make a purchase. Typically, each person pays separately; it is always gracious, though, to treat the person you are meeting. If meeting in a restaurant, be considerate of the need to turn the table, and amply tip the waitstaff.

- For rented or leased space, understand cancellation terms.

Choose the facility options that meet your budget and the needs of your clients and practice.

6 HUMAN RESOURCES

When You are Hired

As a consultant, you can be hired either as an independent contractor or as an employee. This decision is made by your client, based on their assessment of your services and relationship to the organization. The Internal Revenue Service website provides guidance for this determination.

As an independent contractor, you are a separate entity providing service to your client. To help define the relationship, it's highly advisable to get legal assistance and develop a format for a contract or letter of agreement to specify the scope, timing and payment agreed upon between you and your client. As an independent contractor, you are personally responsible for paying all of your tax obligations, on an estimated tax payment schedule. Your client reports the payments made to you to the IRS on a Form 1099.

As an employee, your client becomes your employer, and remits taxes in this capacity. Deductions are made from your payments to cover your portion of the tax liability. The employer reports your income and the taxes remitted to the government on a Form W-2. If you are incorporated, your corporation cannot be classified as an employee.

IF YOU HIRE OTHERS

People you pay to work with or for you can be independent contractors or employees. There are a number of guidelines and rules regarding the differentiation; the Internal Revenue Service has multiple resources available to assist in the decision. MIs-classification of a contractor vs. employee or handling employment informally and/or on a cash basis can result in significant legal exposure and penalties.

Becoming an employer of record requires meeting legal requirements regarding hiring, firing, payroll processing, records maintenance and more. Depending on your needs, a staffing agency arrangement might address much of the complexity and give you the benefits of having employees.

Seek professional advice or work with a reputable agency and handle employment issues appropriately.

Your CEO, COO and Management Skills

Beyond the skills and experience you offer clients, what is your management and entrepreneurial skills set? In your consulting practice, you are the Chief Executive Officer, the Chief Operating Officer and the management team. You are responsible for the direction and control of your company. No one is equally strong in all aspects of business. Identify what you need to learn. You don't need to know every detail in every discipline, but you do need to know the questions to ask, and be able to assess the answers. As your practice grows, complexity will increase. Develop your CEO and COO skills now, and work continually to grow with your business.

- Do you have experience in negotiating contracts, terms and pricing?

- Are you familiar with basic financial operations?

- Are you comfortable establishing and maintaining financial systems, including financial controls, bookkeeping, invoicing and collections?

- Do you have experience in marketing and sales?

- Do you have business networking experience?
- Have you previously managed staff?
- Are you comfortable with public speaking?
- Are you able to write effectively for business?

7 FINANCIAL CONSIDERATIONS

Typical Expenses

You will have both startup and recurring business expenses. Strive to capture them all, and make best estimates regarding their impact.

Typical startup expenses include:

- Legal and related fees for entity formation

- Accountant fees to establish books, including training

- Quickbooks fees

- Registration and/or licensure fees, depending on your area of practice

- Internet and other installation fees
- Website development, technical, graphics and content
- Graphics design for logo
- Initial design for marketing materials
- Hardware: computer, printer/scanner

Recurring expenses include:

- Taxes: Quarterly tax payments
- Rent and utilities, if applicable
- Fees associated with entity renewal
- Accounting and tax preparation fees
- Insurance: business insurance and errors and omissions coverage
- Membership fees: chambers of commerce, networking and leads groups, trade associations
- Event fees: for luncheons, networking events, etc. Typically these are in addition to membership fees and often run from $30 to $35 per event.

- Exposition exhibitor fees: these can run from $100 to $500 or more per event

- Client entertainment

- Promotional items

- Print materials

- Advertising expenses: print and online ads, billboards, radio, etc.

- Travel and mileage

- Telephone and internet charges

- Website hosting and maintenance

- License fees: software, cloud storage, databases, etc.

- Computer antivirus and backup

- Postage, PO Box if used

- Supplies

BUDGETING

Budgeting and projections are critical for getting and keeping your business on track. Take time to think through and develop a sound budget for your business.

- Include both startup and ongoing expenses.

- Remember and plan for periodic expenses such as taxes and insurance payments.

- To calculate the level of billings and collections required to make your target income:
    - Take your total expenses, including pay-backs for startup expenses
    - Add your targeted level of income
    - Divide this by your billable rate
    - This equals the number of hours of work you need to bill and collect to achieve your income goals.

INSURANCE

As a consultant, you have loss and liability exposure.

Basic business risks include things such as fire, theft, and business interruption from catastrophic events. You also have potential liability for occurrences such as injuries sustained by clients while working with you. If you rent facilities for meetings or events, they will typically ask to see proof of your insurance. Even if you see clients in coffee shops or other public venues, you have liability should they slip, fall, or become injured during the course of your meeting.

Professionally, you have additional liability for your actions, including advice you have given, plagiarism or copyright violations. Copyright violations include not only text, but also pictures, graphics and music you may use in conjunction with your practice, or in behalf of a client.

Business insurance is not as straightforward as homeowners' or automobile insurance. Coverage and coverage costs are determined by your industry and scope of services. Your agent needs to be familiar with writing small business insurance, and provide appropriate coverage for your activities and exposure. You don't want to be paying for insurance coverage in excess of your needs, and you especially don't want to believe you are covered for something you are not. Even if you do business from home, your homeowners' policy does not cover liability or loss due to your business. Protect your business and assets and secure appropriate insurance coverage.

Financial Records and Activity

Keep accurate and complete financial records. You need to know where your stand, in order to make reasonable business decisions, and to accurately report and file your income taxes. You can start with something as simple as an excel spreadsheet or utilize a software program such as Quickbooks. In any case, your records are only as good as your diligence in entering data, and in your retention and organization of supporting documents.

- Stay current with your billing, posting, and re-billing activity.

- Anticipate expenses and monitor your cash flow.

- Set payment terms for clients to minimize bad debt exposure. Schedule payments in installments, tied to benchmarks.

- Bill promptly and make every effort to collect promptly. Financial professionals consider any receivables over 60 days old as bad debt. Bad debt is lost money; try to avoid bad debt at all costs.

- Pay your bills on time. Interest on late payments can be significant, and vendors tend to be more responsive to customers who pay promptly.

- If you take out a business loan, meet all loan covenants, and build loan payments into your budget.

- Know your business tax liability. Pay taxes on time. Depending on your location and practice, you may be liable for sales taxes as well as business and self-employment taxes. Insert chapter seven text here. Insert chapter seven text here. Insert chapter seven text here. Insert

8 MARKETING PREPARATION

SET YOUR PROFESSIONAL IMAGE

Everything you do is marketing. This includes the design and color of your logo and materials, the language you use, the way you dress, the social media sites you use, the blogs you write, the professional organizations you join, and more. Keep your message consistent.

Set your image to reflect who you are, your industry, and the clients you serve. You have control over all the variables. Use them to project a memorable and consistent message. What words would you use to describe yourself professionally? Are you dynamic or methodical, innovative or insightful? Your image should support and reinforce your style.

Your logo should reflect your image, in color, theme and style. Online printing companies, website design programs and others often offer stock styles for you to customize and use. Seriously consider hiring a graphic designer or, if this is your skill set, designing a custom logo for yourself. It is confusing and highly embarrassing if someone from another business is found using the same stock logo as yours.

What do your clients expect? Are your business and personal presentation styles consistent with expectations? Usually you want to meet expectations. However, there are conditions in which being a bit unexpected can be a differentiator, make you memorable, and be a strategic advantage. If business casual is the mode, an occasional business formal outfit can be notable. If blogs in your industry feature global market trends, a one time article on the price of sushi is likely to get attention.

Develop Your Product Line

Your product line is a set of offerings to develop and maintain client relationships. Products can include:

- A promotional offering. This may be a free half hour telephone conversation or a downloadable worksheet or a short webinar with immediately applicable content.

- An initial low cost offering. This is an opportunity for someone to see if your services and personality fit their needs.

- Your core product or products. These should be priced at your billable rate, and be the keynote offerings in your marketing campaigns

- Follow-up products. These are products for clients who have purchased your core offerings and want more. These can either be deluxe versions of your keynote offerings or related products and services.

- Premium offerings. These are high end products which deliver high value at a premium price. Premium offerings may resonate with a small percentage of clients, and also serve to highlight the value of you core offerings to your target market.

Set a profile for each product.

- What pain does it relieve?

- Who specifically is the target client?

- How do you deliver this product?

- How much does it cost?

- What is your profit margin?

- What else you can offer this purchaser?

Price your products competitively.

- Research competitors' pricing structures. Check websites and promotional materials.

- See if trade associations have applicable data.

- Ask your business banker if your fee structure seems reasonable.

- Consider your clients' return on investment. Will this purchase create a net benefit in excess of the cost and time invested? What is it worth to your client? Be realistic.

- Consider the profile of your target customers. Are they looking to make small investments for small returns, or do they have the financial capacity and interest to make a major investment for potentially major returns?

You do not need to develop your entire product line before you start; your core product or products should be developed first. The other products should be kept in mind and further developed as interest or demand for them matures.

The Three Decision-Makers

In preparing to market, recognize that there are three potential decision-makers related to a sale. These are the user, they purchaser and the influencer.

The user is the individual who wants and needs your services. They have a pain point that your expertise can relieve. Learn as much as you can about their challenges or problems, what they have tried and what has or has not been effective. What do they want? How will they define a successful outcome? Understand where they are and their vision for success. Define the gap between the two, and position your services to close that gap.

The purchaser approves the purchase and has the budget to pay the bills. This might be the user, but may also be their boss or others within the organization. In a corporate setting, there may be multiple individuals who act together in the role of purchaser. Their interests and concerns can be very different from those of the end user. They might focus on the impact of the engagement on the organization as a whole, any potential repercussions, the cost vs. benefit, and the availability of budgeted funds. As in your discussions with the user, try to identify and address their issues before making your proposal.

The influencer is outside the formal process, but can have a major impact on the purchase decision. The influencer is a respected voice to the user or purchaser. They might be the retired former president of the company, the corporate attorney, a trusted consultant with expertise differing from yours, or their kids' soccer coach. Influencers can serve you as conduits to prospective clients, can affirm the decision to hire your, or can raise issues and questions that cause individuals to reconsider your engagement. Influencers are part of your business network. Develop your relationship to them through your professional outreach and reputation.

9 YOUR MARKETING STRATEGY

To gain engagements, you need to be known, liked and trusted. As a consultant, you are often privy to confidential information, including strategic opportunities and crisis situations. You must be fully trustworthy. Trust is built on familiarity. Your prospective clients must be familiar and comfortable with you professionally. They don't need you to be their best friend forever, but they do need to like you, what you do, and how you do it. And before they like you, they have to meet you and get to know you. Set your strategy to become known, liked and trusted.

BE VISIBLE

Being visible means getting out and making connections. Your goal is to be recognized and remembered as an active member of the business community. Identify and become engaged in the venues where you are likely to meet prospective clients, purchasers and influencers.

- Chambers of commerce and trade associations offer general visibility for you and your consulting practice. Identify organizations whose purpose and members are in line with your services.

- Business expos and trade shows provide opportunities to interact with a number of businesses, as either an exhibitor or attendee. Remember that as an attendee you are there to learn about the offerings of exhibitors; attendees network but do not promote or sell.

- Referral groups consist of non-competing business owners or representatives who met regularly to share leads among members.

- Networking groups may exist within in or independent from chambers of commerce or other organizations. Small businesses are most often represented. Some networking groups are industry-exclusive; most are not.

- What are your interests, hobbies or charitable affiliations? You may find business connections within the groups you currently support. Do not fake an interest in a hobby or passion for a cause just to buttonhole a potential client. This strategy is immediately transparent.

- Making presentations for organizations or conducting your own presentation events can effectively boost visibility. As the presenter, you definitely are noticed by attendees. Professional organizations, chambers of commerce and service organizations are potential hosts and sponsors.

- A self-published book can establish your presence on Amazon, and can provide a relatively inexpensive promotional item. Online soft-ware enables you to do it yourself. If necessary, you can outsource ghost writing, editing, cover design or other components for additional cost.

Be ready to network. Networking is the most direct method to build visibility.

- Have business cards which include your name, business name, contact information and a tag line. Your tag line is a slogan or short statement about your business focus. Have a matte finish on at least one side of the card, with some white space. Give your new acquaintances a place to make a brief note about you on your card. Always have your cards with you. You never know when you might make a useful connection.

- Know your elevator speech. An elevator speech is a brief statement on what you do and what bottom line benefit you can provide to clients.

Years ago, an elevator speech could be two or three minutes long; today with faster elevators and significantly abbreviated attention spans, your elevator speech should be no longer than one or at the most two very short sentences. If people want to know more, they will ask.

- Have a professionally made name tag, and remember to wear it. Your name tag should have your name, business name and logo. The font should be large enough to be easily read, and the print should be in high contrast to the background. Engraved metal name tags might be elegant, but also might be impossible to read.

BE ONLINE

You and your business need to be online. If prospective clients cannot find you through a search, they are likely to assume you and your practice are not legitimate.

A social media presence is a baseline requirement. Depending on your industry and targeted demographics, social media platforms for your business may include LinkedIn, Facebook, Youtube, Instagram, Pinterest, and more.

- Google your name and business name, and review the results. Prospective clients are likely to do an online search; ensure your online presence is professional.

- If you have not already done so, create a personal page and business page on both LinkedIn and Facebook.

- Create accounts on Instagram, YouTube and any other platforms relevant to your industry.

- Post regularly to relevant social media. Photos and videos are important for visibility.

- You must have copyright clearance for any media, including photos, videos and music, that you use. Read the releases; you need clearance for commercial and not just personal use. If there is an identifiable person, a model release is also required.

- React, comment, repost and engage with your online contacts.

- Do not rely on the permanence of any social media platform. You can have thousands of followers on a site, and lose contact with them all if the platform goes out of business or changes their model. Strive to develop a relationship with your audience members, obtain their permission, and capture their email addresses in a compliant email system.

- If you do not have a website, use you LinkedIn business page as your online reference.

A website is highly recommended. A business with only a LinkedIn or Facebook page is at a strategic disadvantage to competitors who elaborate their online presence through dedicated websites. Your website provides a platform to showcase your expertise and provide information about you and your practice. Your website domain name also can be used in your email address and further serve to brand your business.

- Your website should be built on a standardized platform. Ensure that you can transfer hosting and management of your website to a different provider if the need arises.

- Your website should be responsive, and automatically adjust to various devices including tablets and cell phones.

- Obtain all passwords to access your website and related services. Without these, your web developer can hold your website hostage.

- Be able to make changes to your website independently. Information on the site, including blog posts, is subject to constant change and updating. You do not want to be at the mercy of your vendor to make changes in a timely manner, and you do not want to pay for ongoing routine activity.

- Your website can also incorporate a blog. Links to your blog articles can be shared in social media to promote your brand and also direct traffic to your website.

STRATEGIC PARTNERS

Being in business for yourself does not mean going it alone. The right strategic partnerships can accelerate business growth, open new opportunities and potentially save you from disaster.

Unless your expertise lies in these fields, a lawyer and an accountant are important partners as you launch your practice. Setting the right groundwork can help avoid future challenges. Find professionals who work actively in the small business arena.

A small business banker is also an important resource. Beyond the banking relationship, they can often provide insights into market developments and business strategies.

Your fellow consultants can provide guidance in a range of issues, including operations, planning, process improvement, staff management, marketing, sales, social media and more. Small Business Development Centers and SCORE counselors are available in many communities and can provide general information free of charge.

The business world is surprisingly small. Strive to remain on positive professional terms with others, including those you may see as competitors. An apparent competitor might become a strategic partner with skills or a target market complimentary to yours.

Within the business community, seek to build an inner network of individuals who you like and trust, who are experts in their field and who share your core values. These are the people and companies you feel comfortable referring to others, who you trust to deliver outstanding service. As an active consultant, you will be asked for referrals. Your reputation rides on the professionalism of those you recommend. Choose your close associates wisely.

10 BUILDING MOMENTUM AND BEYOND

BUILDING MOMENTUM

Meet and exceed your client's expectations. Ensure you and your client are consistent in expectations regarding the scope of service, time frame, responsiveness, payments, and payment timetables. You may want to work with an attorney to develop a basic boilerplate agreement.

If an engagement is not going well, talk with the client up front and strive to work out the details. If a client is operating in good faith, negotiating price and an early separation of ways may be the best for both parties.

Beware of existing or potential clients who do not intend to operate in good faith. They may complain about your delivery of service, balk at payments, imply they will damage your reputation on social media, or threaten a lawsuit. Keep detailed notes on your discussions and actions with the client, including billable time, your attempts to serve the individual, their broken promises, and other key information. In the event of legal action on their part, this may be of assistance in your defense. A toxic client is not worth keeping. Do your best to terminate the relationship early and as amicably as possible.

Work to retain the good clients you have. Do not ignore them in your scramble to increase your client base. Repeat business is far easier to acquire than new business, and your satisfied clients are your best referral sources.

Your End Game

What is your end game? What do you see as the future of your consulting practice? Is your goal to manage a team of consultants, or continue to work solo? Ultimately, is your goal to merge into another firm, or sell to an associate, or liquidate your practice?

If you have a partnership, have a formal plan for its ultimate end. A partner may develop other interests, or have a different vision for the future. A partner can also become disabled or die. A partnership will always have an end; sometimes happily and amicably, and sometimes contentious or unplanned. Be ready for the inevitable.

As you build your practice, keep your end game in mind. Your ultimate goals may influence decisions regarding your legal form, the clients and industries your serve, the associates you seek, and more. Have your vision and work toward that end.

THE BOTTOM LINE

Taking the leap of faith and launching your own consulting practice can be both exhilarating and intimidating. You are in control, and the master of your fate. You have the capability of doing things your way, and adapting and changing course as you see fit. Every step you make takes you closer to your ideal practice. The steps add up, toward your vision and goals.

Know when you can use help, and get the help you need. You will have more than enough to do without struggling to master a new range of technical skills. Lawyers, accountants, marketers, social media pros, small business advisors, IT specialists and more spend their professional lives concentrating on one aspect of business. What can take you hours to do might be only a quick few minutes of work for them. Invest in expertise, both in starting up and in growing your business.

The rate of change is accelerating. It is unlikely that you will have 100% of the information you need to make any decision with 100% certainty. Under these conditions, the strategy of "ready, fire, aim" becomes critical. Think through your plans, do your research, and take your best shot. If your aim is off, adjust and try again. Sometimes the best way to find your shortfalls and miscalculations is to launch and learn.

An independent consulting practice is challenging and crazy, fun and frustrating. If you choose to take the leap, whatever the outcome, whether you embrace this as your new career path or dabble in the field, whether you return to the corporate world or create a new entrepreneurial empire, you will never have to say, "I wonder what would have happened if I struck out on my own?"

Embrace your vision. Welcome aboard the roller-coaster, and enjoy the ride!

ABOUT THE AUTHOR

Ellen Huxtable is a business growth strategist, speaker, author and facilitator. She founded her consulting practice, Advantage Business Concepts, over fifteen years ago. She is the author of three other books, "Power Networking for Job Seekers," "Power Networking for Small Businesses," and "Turbo-charge & Transform!" a workbook for transformative business innovation. She is the host of Batavia Spotlight, a business program on BATV public access television. Ellen is a member of the Fermilab Community Advisory Board and the Board of Directors for the Cavaliers Drum and Bugle Corps. Ellen holds an MBA from the Kellogg Graduate School of Management, Northwestern University.

www.ingramcontent.com/pod-product-compliance
Lightning Source LLC
Chambersburg PA
CBHW070828220526
45466CB00002B/776